A Special Gift

Presented to:

....

From:

....

Date:

....

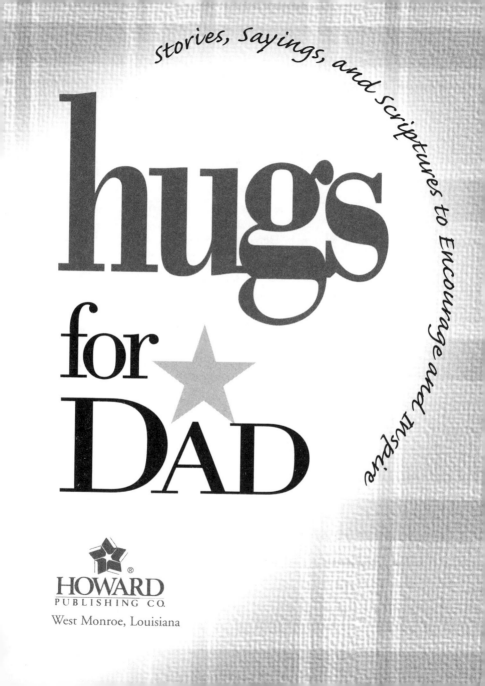

Stories, sayings, and scriptures to Encourage and Inspire

hugs
for ★
DAD

HOWARD
PUBLISHING CO.

West Monroe, Louisiana

Our purpose at Howard Publishing is:

- *Increase faith* in the hearts of growing Christians
- *Inspire holiness* in the lives of believers
- *Instill hope* in the hearts of struggling people
  everywhere

Because He's coming again!

Hugs for Dad © 1997 by Howard Publishing Co., Inc.
All rights reserved. Printed in the United States of America
Published by Howard Publishing Co., Inc.,
3117 North 7th Street, West Monroe, LA 71291-2227

02 03 04 05 06   20 19 18 17 16

Stories by John William Smith, author of *My Mother's Favorite Song,*
My Mother Played the Piano, and contributor to other *Hugs* books

Paraphrased Scriptures © 2000 LeAnn Weiss, 3006 Brandywine Dr.,
Orlando, FL 32806; 407-898-4410

Jacket Design and Interior Art by LinDee Loveland
Edited by Philis Boultinghouse

The first printing was catalogued as follows:
Library of Congress Cataloging-in-Publication Data

Hugs for the heart for dad : stories, sayings, and scriptures to
    encourage and inspire
        p. cm.
    ISBN 1-878990-70-5 (alk. paper)
    1. Fathers—Religious life. 2. Fatherhood—Religious
aspects—Christianity. I. Howard Publishing Co.
BV4529.H836 1997
242'.6421—dc21   97-680
                                                                CIP

Contents

one

Making
History

Dad, your children are watching you! They see and hear what you tell them and what you model to them through your life. Don't hide me from them. Tell them of all of the praiseworthy things I've done throughout history and in your life. Tell them of my power and my wonders. Teach them to put their trust in me and not to forget my commandments. In turn, they will teach and model them to their children. You are making history!

Love,

Your 100% Faithful Heavenly Father

Psalm 78:3–8

There's something in a man that makes him want to be a history-maker – a *hero*. Most men grow up with grand ideas of accomplishing great things. They hold visions of rescuing lives threatened by fire, winning major battles in a war, influencing the laws of the land through public office, defending the underdog in a court case, or finding a cure for cancer. They have a hungry ambition to be a hero who shapes the future.

Well, Dad, that's just what you are. Your heroics may not be recorded in a best-selling novel, a classic movie, or on the cover of a magazine, but your actions are recorded frequently in the hearts and minds of your children. They record your simple, but heroic, deeds every day.

They have pictures in their minds of you smiling in a way that communicated how proud you were of them. They remember the times you wiped tears from their red and swollen faces and offered words of comfort. They recall how attentively you listened to them share their pain over failed romances or disappointing failures. They review pictures of scrimmages in the driveway, dates for dinner, visits to school, unexpected gifts, and loving hugs. They remember your praying posture beside their bed and the life-changing instructions that came from your lips.

You are a history-maker and a future-shaper of the most important kind. You live on the front pages of the hearts of those you love the most.

The best things you
can give children, next
to good habits, are
good memories.

—Sydney Harris

Jump

One day I was playing in our backyard with a paint can lid. It was before the days of Frisbees – perhaps the inventor of the Frisbee got his idea from watching the creative genius of a child who, like me, had discovered the amazing flying propensities of a paint can lid. I was sailing it into the wind, and as its momentum slowed, the wind would take it higher and higher and then it would begin its downward and backward glide, and I would try to catch it. Eventually it landed and lodged on the roof of the chicken coop. I fretted and worried most of the afternoon trying to dislodge it. We had no ladder, and I finally gave up.

When my father came home, I met him in the driveway. Before he was out of the car, I began pleading with him to help me retrieve my toy. He put his lunch pail down on the front porch, and we walked around the house together. He assured me that it was no problem and that we could get it back.

★

I jumped – with no hesitation. I jumped, and he caught me easily and hugged me and then swung me to the ground.

He hoisted me up on his shoulders – then grabbed my feet and boosted me up onto the roof of the chicken coop. He told me to walk very carefully because the coop was old and decaying. I retrieved my toy and returned to the edge of the coop. I felt very powerful looking down at my father. He smiled up at me and then held out his arms and said,

"Jump."

I close my eyes and I can see him now, forty-five years later, as plainly as I can see the lake and the trees from where I sit just now. He was so tall, so strong, so confident with his big, handsome, grinning face, that it is easier for me to imagine that day than the day he died.

I jumped – with no hesitation. I jumped, and he caught me easily and hugged me and then swung me to the ground.

He sent me to get his lunch pail, and in a moment we were in the house and the incident was forgotten – no, it wasn't forgotten, was it? He would be amazed that I remember it – I'm sure that within a very short time, he forgot it. He wasn't trying consciously to be a good father. He didn't come home that day with a plan to create a lasting memory for his son. It wasn't planned at all.

★

Many great opportunities for lasting impressions are either lost or become negatives because you can't fake what you are when the unexpected comes.

My point to you parents is that most parenting cannot be planned – except in your own personal walk

Making History

with God and in prayer. Many great opportunities for lasting impressions are either lost or become negatives because you can't fake what you are when the unexpected comes.

★

We become good parents – good neighbors, good husbands, and good friends – by becoming good, by turning our lives toward God.

If my father had generally been selfishly unconcerned with his children's cares, there would have been no time or cause for him to turn this unexpected moment into a great triumph – he would have acted according to his nature, told me he was much too tired to fool with me, reprimanded me for my carelessness, and gone into the house leaving me to my own devices – and the moment would have been lost.

The opportunities come – unexpectedly, unplanned for – and most of the time we react according to our nature. We serve our children best by seeking to constantly become more closely molded into the image of our Lord Jesus Christ. We do not become good parents by trying to practice a parenting philosophy that is contrary to our natures. We become good parents – good neighbors, good husbands, and good friends – by becoming *good,*

by turning our lives toward God.

reflections . . .

two

Leading Your Family

Remember, you are not alone in the awesome responsibility of leading your family. I go ahead of you on your journey of life. I search out your options and show you the way you should go. In the difficult places of life, I carry you as a father carries his son. I faithfully guide you all the way! The key to success is trusting me and teaching your children by your example the importance of following me wholeheartedly.

Love,

The Lord Your God,

Who Goes Before You

Deuteronomy 1:30–36

Have you heard the story about the little child who is walking with Dad through the woods?

They'd been walking for several hours, and the end of the woods was nowhere in sight. Dad stopped to survey the area and assess their situation. There were no signs of civilization. No houses, no gas stations, no convenience stores, no cars.

Dad playfully asked the child, "Which way should we go?"

"I don't know, Dad, I've never been this way before."

"Are you saying that you're lost?" asked the dad.

"How could I be lost?" the child responded. "I'm following you!"

Dad, whether you know it or not, you are being followed. No matter your age, there will always be younger legs trying to walk in the imprints you've made. But leading your family is not as lonely a job as it may seem. For you have one who has gone before you to show the way. Your family can confidently follow you, as you follow Christ.

So lead on, Dad. Lead your family to the summits of life. Lead them through the frightening shadows with bold bravery. Model a resolute faith that the light will overcome the dark. Ignore the whispering voices that urge compromise, and stand strong on your convictions. Climb every mountain with confidence in Christ to give you strength. Fall to your knees and pray when your family stumbles through the valley. Feed your soul and the souls of your family with uplifting fellowship. Expose the traps of Satan with the light of the Word. Grapple bravely with tough decisions using the gift of spiritual wisdom. Focus your eyes on the peak and push ahead through the rocky canyons.

Remember – you are not alone. You have one who has gone before you to show the way.

Your family has never been this way before, but they won't get lost as long as they follow you and follow Him.

Lead on, Dad.

By profession I am a soldier and take pride in that fact. But I am prouder—infinitely prouder—to be a father. A soldier destroys in order to build; the father only builds, never destroys. It is my hope that my son, when I am gone, will remember me not from the battle but in the home repeating with him our simple daily prayer, "Our Father Who Art in Heaven."

—General Douglas MacArthur

The
Upward Way

The boy was short, and he still had quite a bit of "baby fat." He wore glasses and was often teased. His school record was far from brilliant – except that he was favored by his teachers because he was well mannered and said, "Sir" and "Ma'am." His father and mother were concerned because he had no victories. He lacked aggressiveness, and he seemed to be constantly withdrawn. He had little enthusiasm for life, and he was alone much.

Behind their house were some high mountains topped by great jagged upthrusts of perpendicular rock. The steep slopes beneath were extremely rugged

Leading Your Family

and forbidding and were covered with pin oak brush, cat claw, cactus, manzanita, ironwood, and ponderosa pine – with an occasional blue spruce. The washes, which carried the spring runoff, cut deep ravines in these slopes and were choked with huge boulders – which had fallen ages ago – fallen trees, brush, and other debris. The father noticed that the boy looked often toward those craggy summits, gazing long minutes in wonder at their majesty. One winter day, when the sun was glistening radiantly from the snow-covered peaks, the boy expressed his desire to someday climb to the top. The father determined that his chance would come.

★

One winter day, when the sun was glistening radiantly from the snow-covered peaks, the boy expressed his desire to someday climb to the top. The father determined that his chance would come.

Accordingly, one fine spring day – with no warning – the father announced that there would be no school that day — a special project was planned. The excitement, the anticipation — as they filled canteens, packed a lunch, and dressed appropriately in *climbing clothes* — lit the boys face and put a fire in his eyes that the father had rarely seen. They drove up the mountain as far as the last rut-riddled road would take them, found a promising ravine, and set out.

★

The father had not realized how difficult a task he had set, but he knew they must not fail; the boy must accomplish this.

Those who mounted Everest worked no harder, suffered no greater hardship or discouragement — and had no greater desire to quit. The father had not realized how difficult a task he had set, but he knew they must not fail; the boy must accomplish this. The boy — red-faced from exertion, panting hoarsely, sweating profusely — hinted more than once that perhaps they ought to return.

But the heroic ascent continued.

Leading Your Family

Finally, they broke out into the open, and the panorama of the miles they could see was awesome. Their whole town, tucked away in a fold of lesser hills, looked insignificant. "I'll bet we can see Flagstaff from the top," the boy cried – and they plunged ahead.

When they came to a second opening, they stopped and ate part of their lunch. They rested their weary backs and aching legs against a great ponderosa. They shared a tree, a sandwich, a canteen, a view, a struggle, a hope, their fatigue – and they shared the marvelous silence.

"It sure is quiet, isn't it, Dad? I never heard it so quiet before."

They were close, and it was good.

There was no talk of returning now. When they finally, reluctantly – but with renewed vigor – left their lunch spot, they only talked of how long – how far to the top. The last seventy-five yards was hand over hand climbing up a vertical, rock-ribbed surface. When they reached the top, their hearts were pounding and they were absolutely breathless. The father came behind – to help the boy, to reassure him against falling, and because he wanted him to be first. When the boy finally topped the ascent, he paused and turned, stretching out his hands, his long brown hair moving with the wind – some of it sticking to the sweat of his forehead – and he said,

"Let me help you up, Dad. It's great."

★

The father came behind – to help the boy, to reassure him against falling, and because he wanted him to be first.

Even here, although a basic plan was made, there could be no preparation for what might possibly happen along the way – because the father had not made the trip before. We can purpose to do good, but the actual doing is always a reaction to the providential opportunities which He affords.

reflections . . . .

_____

_____

_____

_____

_____

_____

_____

_____

_____

_____

_____

_____

three

Experiencing Victory

Life isn't always easy! Teach your children to look at obstacles from my perspective and to remember that they can do all things because I strengthen them. Remind them that my absolute power is made perfect in their weakness. Teach them to see failures, hardships, persecutions, and difficult circumstances as opportunities for my power to work in supernatural ways.

Love,

Your God of Victory

Philippians 4:13
2 Corinthians 12:9–10

If you look up the word *triumph* in the thesaurus, you'll find words like *victory, win, achievement,* and *conquest.* You'll also find words like *joy, celebrate, jubilation,* and *rejoice.* Then, if you look up *fail* or *failure,* you'll find *defeat, ineffectiveness, fault,* and *inferiority;* and you'll also find *wither, collapse,* and, of course, *disappointment.*

These word associations from the thesaurus are merely reflections of how our society views success and failure. No wonder so many children feel that winning is all important and that failure is unacceptable. And since all of us fail at being perfect parents, spouses, children, friends, and Christians, we are set up for a pretty miserable existence. But it doesn't have to be that way. God never intended it to be so.

Christ did not die for us when we were winners. In fact, God's Word says that "at just the right time, when we were still *power-less,* Christ died for the ungodly." God, our heavenly Father, sent Jesus "at just the right time" – when we

were powerless . . . failures . . . last place finish-
ers. What a great lesson for us as earthly fathers.
When our children lose the contest, fail the exam, or
fall on their way to the finish line, that's when they
need our very best – they need us to imitate our heavenly Father and love them when they fail. They need
warm hugs to renew self-esteem, raised arms at the finish
line (even if they finish last), pats on the back, and words
of affirmation at the final horn – no matter the outcome.
They need to know it's all right to fail, for they will do
plenty of that in this life.

Dad, you can rewrite the thesaurus. You can
teach your sons and daughters that there is *pride* in
trying, *celebration* in participating, *joy* in simply
running the race. Add some new words under
the word failure. Add words like *acceptance,
encouragement, renewal,* and *hope.* "At just
the right time" – when they have failed
– teach them of the victory we have
in Jesus.

*I*t's not whether
you get knocked
down, it's whether
you get up.

—Vince Lombardi

The Winner

I was watching some little kids play soccer. I don't have little ones anymore, so I just watch them – and their parents. These kids were about five or six. They were playing a real game – a serious game – two teams, complete with coaches, uniforms, and parents. I didn't know any of them, so I was able to enjoy the game without the distraction of being anxious about winning or losing –

I wished the parents and coaches
could have done the same.

The teams were pretty evenly matched. I will just call them Team One and Team Two. Nobody scored in the first period. The kids were hilarious. They were

Experiencing Victory

clumsy and terribly inefficient. They fell over their own feet, they stumbled over the ball, they kicked at the ball and missed it – but they didn't seem to care.

They were having fun.

★

He was an outstanding athlete, but he was no match for three or four boys who were also very good.

In the second quarter, the Team One coach pulled out what must have been his first team and put in the scrubs, except for his best player who now guarded the goal. The game took a dramatic turn. I guess winning is important – even when you're five years old – because the Team Two coach left his best players in, and the Team One scrubs were no match for them. Team Two swarmed around the little guy who was now the Team One goalie. He was an outstanding athlete, but he was no match for three or four boys who were also very good. Team Two began to score.

The Winner

The lone goalie gave it everything he had, recklessly throwing his body in front of incoming balls, trying to stop them. Team Two scored two goals in quick succession. It infuriated the young boy. He became a raging maniac—shouting, running, diving. With all the stamina he could muster, he covered the boy who now had the ball; but that boy kicked it to another boy twenty feet away, and by the time he repositioned himself, it was too late – they scored a third goal.

I soon learned who his parents were. They were nice, decent-looking people. I could tell that his dad had just come from the office – he still had his suit and tie on. They yelled encouragement to their son. I became totally absorbed, watching the boy on the field and his parents on the sidelines.

After the third goal, the little kid changed. He could see it was no use; he couldn't stop them. He didn't quit, but he became quietly desperate –

futility was written all over him.

His father changed too. He had been urging his son to try harder – yelling advice and encouragement. But then he changed. He became anxious. He tried to say that it was okay, to hang in there. He grieved for the pain his son was feeling.

After the fourth goal, I knew what was going to happen. I've seen it before. The little boy needed help so badly, and there was no help to be had. He retrieved the ball from the net and handed it to the referee – and then he cried. He just stood there while huge tears rolled down both cheeks. He went to his knees and put his fists to his eyes – and he cried the tears of the helpless and brokenhearted.

★

When the boy went to his knees, I saw the father start onto the field. His wife clutched his arm and said, "Jim, don't. You'll embarrass him." But he tore loose from her and ran onto the field.

When the boy went to his knees, I saw the father start onto the field. His wife clutched his arm and said, "Jim, don't. You'll embarrass him." But he tore loose

The Winner

from her and ran onto the field. He wasn't supposed to
– the game was still in progress. Suit, tie, dress shoes,
and all – he charged onto the field, and he picked up
his son so everybody would know that this was his boy,
and he hugged him and held him and cried with him.
I've never been so proud of a man in my life.

★

"Daddy," the boy sobbed, "I couldn't stop
them. I tried, Daddy, I tried and tried,
and they scored on me."

He carried him off the field, and when he got close
to the sidelines I heard him say, "Scotty, I'm so proud
of you. You were great out there. I want everybody to
know that you are my son."

"Daddy," the boy sobbed, "I couldn't stop them. I
tried, Daddy, I tried and tried, and they scored on me."

"Scotty, it doesn't matter how many times they
scored on you. You're my son, and I'm proud of you. I
want you to go back out there and finish the game. I
know you want to quit, but you can't. And, son, you're

going to get scored on again, but it doesn't matter. Go on, now."

It made a difference – I could tell it did. When you're all alone, and you're getting scored on – and you can't stop them – it means a lot to know that it doesn't matter to those who love you. The little guy ran back on to the field – and they scored two more times –

but it was okay.

★

I get scored on every day. I try so hard. I recklessly throw my body in every direction. I fume and rage. I struggle with temptation and sin – and Satan laughs.

I get scored on every day. I try so hard. I recklessly throw my body in every direction. I fume and rage. I struggle with temptation and sin – and Satan laughs. And he scores again, and the tears come, and I go to my knees – sinful, convicted, helpless. And my Father – my Father rushes right out on the field – right in

The Winner

front of the whole crowd – the whole jeering, laughing world – and he picks me up, and he hugs me and he says, "John, I'm so proud of you. You were great out there. I want everybody to know that you are my son, and because I control the outcome of this game, I declare you –

The Winner."

reflections . . . .

_____

_____

_____

_____

_____

_____

_____

_____

_____

_____

_____

_____

four

Creating
Independence

Your children are going to make mistakes and will stumble and fall at times. Teach them the secret of *empowerment*. When they wait upon me and put their hope in me, they will renew their strength. They will be able to soar through life's storms on wings like eagles. By tapping into my unlimited power, they will be able to "run" through life without growing weary.

Love,

Your God of Hope and Power

Isaiah 40:29–31

You rock them as infants, play hide and seek with them as toddlers, and send them off for their first day of school. You sit on hard bleachers watching hours of ball games and school plays; you agonize with them over algebra; you hurt with them through dating disappointments and swell with pride as they prepare for graduation night – you invest so much. And then, you find out, you have to let them go!

Seeing those first signs of independence can be rough on a dad. It starts with little things. Your daughter may begin by deciding to wear her yellow dress instead of the blue one you said looked better on her; your son may choose to play soccer instead of baseball, when you thought softball was obviously the better choice. But it doesn't stop there.

Pretty soon they're deciding who to date and where to go to college. It's not easy on a dad. But isn't that your whole purpose in parenting – to bring your children to the point where they can make it on their own? As a nurturing dad, you

impart to your children both roots and wings –
roots that grow deep in the soil of family traditions
and unconditional love, and wings that empower your
growing children to rise from your home and fly with
strength and courage on a course of their own.

When the fledgling, almost-adult child, first begins to
fly, it's inevitable that there be some false starts – even some
crash landings. Less-than-wise financial decisions, disappointing romances, difficult career choices – such things
cause dads to doubt themselves and children to want to
run back to the safety of home.

But it's all a part of the process we call growing up.
And when those seeds of independence begin to grow
and your children become responsible young women
and men with convictions and dreams of their
own, you'll know a little of the pride your heavenly Father feels when he sees his children
soar above the confines of this world on
wings of faith.

There are only two lasting bequests we can hope to give our children. One of these is roots, the other wings.

—Hodding Carter

She's All Right

It nearly always comes at night, and most of the time it comes very late. I had been asleep for some time when the phone rang. I fumbled clumsily in the dark for the receiver – knocking the Kleenex box onto the floor, then tipping the lamp over. Muttering under my breath that if this was a wrong number or a solicitation of some sort – somebody was going to get an earful. I finally found the phone and mumbled a very unfriendly, "Hello." A few apprehensive seconds of silence followed – and then this sound:

"Dad!"

Just the one word – I was fully awake. My reply was instantaneous.

"Kris? – What's wrong?"

Creating Independence

The next sound I heard is known to every parent – every person. From the cradle to the grave – it is the universal sound of heartbreak. She had held it as long as she could – long enough to make the call – because there is only one thing worse than grieving, and that's grieving alone.

★

The next sound I heard is known to every parent – every person. From the cradle to the grave – it is the universal sound of heartbreak.

Her grief was so intense that she could not speak. All I could do was listen – and grieve with her – and dread. The list of potential explanations was not comforting: disease, drugs, pregnancy, failing grades, dismissal from school, death or injury to someone close to us. The sobbing subsided, temporarily, and the story began to come out. Haltingly, she told me that she had broken up with her boyfriend – not *just* a boyfriend,

She's All Right

but a boy she had given her heart to and had hoped to marry – a boy she loved. She was devastated – I was relieved.

> "Thank God," I thought –
> "It's only that."

She vented her frustration – because she didn't understand; her anger – because she felt betrayed; and her loneliness and isolation – because it was her first time and because she thought she was the only one. And as she talked, I realized what *distance* means – we were so far apart – and how little, practically, that I could do.

★

"Can I come home?" she said. "Dad, I just want to be in my own room and sleep in my own bed. Please – let me come home."

"Can I come home?" she said. "Dad, I just want to be in my own room and sleep in my own bed."

"Please – let me come home."

Creating Independence

Oh, my dearest child, I thought, how I know what you're feeling – how I understand how a broken heart turns toward *home*. What a compliment to your mother and I that at the hour of your greatest need, you have remembered home – and turned to us. You need healing – and the balm of home is the only healing you know. But, my dearest, the world will not go away, and not even home can provide the medication you need. That is what I thought, but I said –

"Of course, you can come home.
Mom and I would love to see you."

But even as I said it, my mind was leaping from the present to the future. I was aware of how much I *wanted* her to come home – how badly I *wanted* to provide the answers – to sooth and smooth and approve her. I *wanted* her to depend on me – to find her center in us – and even then, I knew that what *I* wanted – needed – was not what *she* needed. I knew that if she came home now – she would come home again – and again. And so I said,

She's All Right

"What would you do here, honey? You have no friends here – nothing to occupy your time. Mom and I would have to work. What would you do all day?"

"I don't know, Dad. I just don't know what to do."

"I don't know either, but it seems to me that you would be very lonesome – and eventually, you'd have to go back. Wouldn't it be easier to face it now? You know you would have to go back – don't you?"

★

Oh, my love, my baby, my darling girl – all things are so real for you in this moment – it is a cruel world after all. And now I was crying.

"I hadn't thought about that," she said – as though it was just now occurring to her that *her* world was the only one that had crashed and that even a crashed world would not prevent tomorrow. We talked on and on – and even as we talked – she grew up a little. New realities were making lasting impressions.

Creating Independence

"I guess there's no more coming home for me.
Is there, Dad?"

It was an aching question, and I ached in reply; but I was glad that *she* had asked it.

"No, Kris. There's no more coming home."

Oh, my love, my baby, my darling girl – all things are so real for you in this moment – it is a cruel world after all.

And now I was crying.

We both knew that she was beyond my healing – that even home, familiar walls, her own bed, and our love were not enough to replace the emptiness that was in her heart. We were overwhelmed by our helplessness and our dependence.

"Dad, will you and Mom pray for me?"

"We always do."

"But, would you especially pray for me right now. It's the only hope I have."

Yes, it is the only hope we have ever had, but it takes times like these to realize it. She would forget – but the next time her heart breaks, she would remember more

She's All Right

easily and she would turn in that direction more completely – and some day – when her mom and I are gone – that will truly be her only hope and refuge.

"I'll be all right now, Dad. Don't worry."

Yes, I thought, you'll be all right – not as you mean it, but you will be all right. Of course, that won't keep us from worrying – it's never that easy.

"I love you, Dad – more than ever."

"I love you too."

★

"I love you, Dad – more than ever."

It was not the same thing – her love and mine – but it was closer than it had ever been – much closer. *I* hadn't moved much – but she had made a quantum leap.

I hung up and my wife – who was wide awake – said, "Is she all right?" It's tough – hearing half a conversation.

"Yes, honey, she's all right – in fact, she's more all right than she's been in some time, but the next few weeks are going to be tough."

65

Creating Independence

"Is she coming home?"

"No, she's not coming home. We've lost our baby.
She's becoming – what we raised her to be –

she's all right."

I wouldn't want to do it again – raise my kids, I
mean, but doing it has created a wonder – an under-
standing and a sense of dependence on God that I
would never have had without it.

reflections . . .

five

Being There

As my Father has loved me, so I have loved you! Remain in my love. You are able to love your family because I first loved you! Show them your love by being there for them like I'm always here for you. Let me turn your heart to your children and their hearts to you!

Love always and forever,

Jesus

John 15:9
Malachi 4:6

Being there for the big moments is really quite accidental. It happens because you've been there for the everyday, mundane moments. Big moments take us by surprise. Rarely are they planned for; rarely can we predict them. They just happen.

And so in order to be there for the momentous moments, you have to be there for the inconsequential ones. If you want to be there for the basketball game where your daughter scores twenty points, you have to be there when she sits on the bench. In order to be there when your son is ready to talk about a serious struggle with temptation, you have to be there when he wants to gripe about how hard his English teacher is. In order to be there for your daughter's first romantic rejection,

you must be there when she chatters about
what everybody's wearing.

Being there doesn't mean knowing exactly what
to say. It doesn't mean having all the answers or promising a perfect future. It doesn't mean being the smartest or
the richest or the funniest or the strongest. It means simply being with the ones who depend on you. It means
investing time in the ordinary events of your children's
lives, so that when the big moments come – the
moments that impact their future – you'll be right
there in position – right where you are needed.

Isn't that one of the things you appreciate
most about your heavenly Father? He's always
there – not just for the big times, but for
the small times too. You can imitate
your heavenly Father by simply
being there.

Nothing I've ever done
has given me more joys
and rewards than being a
father to my children.

—Bill Cosby

Love's Old Sweet Song

Just a song at twilight,
When the lights are low
And the flickering shadows
Come and softly go.
When the heart is weary,
Sad the day and long,
Still to us at twilight
Comes love's old sweet song.
—G. Clifton Bingham

During the year that we lived on Gardenia Street in Royal Oak, I got very sick. I think it was some sort of influenza, but the Smith's didn't *doctor* much, so we never knew. We accepted our sicknesses as a part of God's divine providence, and we worked our way

Being There

through them as best we could. We cured everything with chicken noodle soup, dry toast, poached eggs, and hot tea – and of course, there were cold washcloths for fever.

I had been sick for several days, and my vomiting, fever, and inability to eat or drink had made me very weak. My mother had stayed at my bedside, or close by, the entire time. My dad was working at some kind of tool and die shop, so I only saw him in the evenings. He would stick his head in the door to see if I was awake. If I was, he'd grin real big and say, "Hey, Bud, how you doing?" He said it so cheerfully that it made me feel better. That was at first.

★

Toward the end, I was so sick and weak that I could scarcely speak – and they had begun to worry.

Toward the end, when I was so sick and weak that I could scarcely speak and they had begun to worry, he'd come in and take my hand or rumple my hair a little, and he'd say, "How you feeling, Son?" His face would be filled with care, and I was sorry to worry him so.

One night, very late, I awoke slowly from my feverish sleep. The light was on in the hallway and the door to my room was open just a crack. In the shadowy half-light I could see someone sitting by my bed. I thought it was my mother. I must have moved a little, because I felt someone squeeze my hand. Then I knew it wasn't my mother. The hand was large, strong and rough. Without turning my head, I moved my eyes slowly in his direction. He was sitting – slumped over in a chair. He still had his work clothes on – a light blue shirt and dark blue pants with heavy black shoes and white socks. There were stains on the shirt, and it had that kind of burned-oil smell that saturated all of his shop uniforms. His head was resting in his hand, his eyes were closed, and there were tears on his face. When I saw his lips move a little, I knew immediately that he was praying.

My dad was singing "Love's Old Sweet Song" – not those words and not music, you understand – but the oldest, sweetest song there is – a song that has been sung since the beginning of time. My dad was singing it at its very best. I was eleven.

Being There

What I want you to see is that his presence paid – more than paid – for all of his failures. Fathers can fail much and often – and they do – even the best of them. But when the big moments come – the real crises – they have to be there.

★

His head was resting in his hand, his eyes were closed, and there were tears on his face. When I saw his lips move a little, I knew immediately that he was praying.

And this is really important: You never know when the big moments will come. You can't just show up for the big moments. You have to show up every day and be there for all of the little moments – the ones that don't get remembered – that's the price you pay to get to be there when that providential opportunity presents itself –

to create a memory.

Sometimes you have to fail a thousand times to succeed just once. And when you do succeed, that big success becomes the climax to the failures. And the failures aren't really failures anymore – they're just the parental training ground – and even a child understands that you have to practice and that if you don't, you strike out with the bases loaded.

Being there consistently is the only guarantee of being there when those moments come.

Remember, one of God's most impressive qualities is that

> he is the God
> who is *there*.

reflections . . . .

six

Instilling Values

Some foolishness is bound up in the heart of every child. Don't give in. Don't neglect the responsibility I've given you to correct and instill my values in your children. Let my Word dwell in you richly as you teach and admonish them with all my unlimited wisdom.

Love,
Your Father Whose Ways Are
Much Higher Than Yours

Proverbs 22:15
Colossians 3:12

You're the kind of father who knows how to take a stand. You've bucked the trends; you've swum against the current; you've fought invisible enemies; you've stood your ground in the face of severe opposition. That's the kind of father you are.

Because you know how to take a stand, because you hold to a strong value system, you've earned what most men truly desire but never receive – you've earned *respect* and *love*. Your family has given you these two gifts freely and willingly. But these gifts have come at great price.

You've paid the price of *rejection* when you made an unpopular decision. It would have been so much easier to give in and quiet the protests. Instead, you took the heat and hearts were changed. That's the kind of father you are.

You've absorbed the loss of *peace* when selfishness and sin needed to be rebuked. You could have

simply ignored the fatal symptoms. Instead, you
lovingly confronted and averted catastrophe. That's
the kind of father you are.

You've surrendered *security* to teach responsibility
behind the wheel. You've contributed coveted *evenings* to
support endless events and encourage the growth of timid
talents. You've sacrificed *sleep* to pray for God's protection
when your family was under attack.

Oh . . . that explains it. That's why you're the kind of
father you are. You depend on his strength not yours –
his resolve, not your own – his determination, his wisdom, his love. You're willing to make the sacrifices
you do because you understand the great price that
your Father paid to take care of you. He sacrificed all so that you could live. That's the
kind of Father he is – and that's why
you're the kind of father you are.
That's why you're so loved.

Responsibility is the
thing people dread most
of all. Yet it is the one
thing in the world that
develops us, gives us
manhood . . . fibre.

—Frank Crane

Which Kind Are You?

Judi went into the Winn-Dixie to buy a few items we needed. It was totally dark, and it was raining. I parked where I could see both store exits, so that when she came out, I could pick her up. For this time of night there were a lot of shoppers. I opened my window about three inches to keep it from fogging.

There was a Chevy station wagon parked pretty close to me, and as I waited, the family who owned it came out. They had their sacks of groceries in a shopping cart. There were five of them. The husband and wife were about thirty-five – he was pudgy and balding, she was sort of plain vanilla – except for her hair. The rain and the gentle glow of the vapor lights in the parking lot caused it to shine nice and soft, and it curled all over her head and neck and down into her

Instilling Values

face. I wanted to tell her how pretty it was, but I didn't. They had a boy – about ten, I guess. He was pushing the cart. He looked like most ten-year-old boys – jeans, T-shirt and Reeboks. There were also two nondescript children – about four and six, maybe, but their gender will forever remain a mystery.

The father opened the tailgate of the station wagon, and he and the boy unloaded the cart. When they finished, the father said, "Run the cart over there to the collecting area, Danny."

It was raining – but not hard – it wasn't offensive, just a sort of warm, pleasant drizzle that makes you want a good book, someone you love, and the leisure to be drowsy.

★

"It will only take a second, and it won't hurt you." But there was no conviction in his voice.

The boy didn't want to. They were about forty yards from me. I could hear them plainly, and I'm sure they never noticed me.

Which Kind Are You?

"Aw, Dad; it's raining," he complained.

"It will only take a second, and it won't hurt you." But there was no conviction in his voice; the father was reasoning with the boy – treating him as an equal.

The boy took full advantage.

"Those people over there didn't put theirs back," he argued, pointing to several carts carelessly left in various places.

★

"For heaven's sake, Carl, come on! One more cart in the parking lot won't change the history of the world."

"We're not responsible for them, just for us," the father rejoined.

"But who cares?" the boy replied. They got people hired to come out here and collect these carts."

The mother, tired of waiting, now joined in on the boy's side.

Instilling Values

"For heaven's sake, Carl, come on! One more cart in the parking lot won't change the history of the world."

★

The boy sensed victory and opened the door to get in. The father shrugged his shoulders in defeat and put his hand on the door handle. Then he stopped.

The boy sensed victory and opened the door to get in. The father shrugged his shoulders in defeat and put his hand on the door handle. Then he stopped. At first I couldn't figure out why, but I followed his eyes across the misty parking lot and I saw what he saw – an elderly couple, her arm in his, pushing their cart slowly toward the collection area. It caused a whole transformation in him. His posture straightened, his chin lifted, and his shoulders squared a little. I suspect he looked much like the man he had been when he got married. And when he spoke, there was firmness and authority in his voice.

"Danny", he said, "come here."

Which Kind Are You?

Danny came.

"Do you see those carts that are *in* the cart collecting area? Danny, there are two kinds of people – those who put their carts away and those who don't. In this family, Danny, we put our carts away – because that's the kind of people we are. Don't ever forget that. Now put that cart where it belongs."

★

There are two kinds of people in every area of life – two kinds of people – two kinds of fathers.

As the boy directed the cart to its appropriate place, it occurred to me how right the father was. There are two kinds of people in every area of life – two kinds of people – two kinds of fathers.

Which kind are you?

reflections . . . .

seven

Learning Humility

Follow me by descending into greatness: Model humility to your children. Remember, I oppose the proud, but I give my amazing grace to those who are humble. Pride and self-ishness only puff your ego up, but love builds your children up!

Love,

Jesus

1 Peter 5:5

1 Corinthians 8:1

I'm going to tell you a

secret that will make you feel a whole lot better about yourself. It's something you've
allowed yourself to consider before . . . but not
for very long.

The very essence of this secret will make
you bristle, even though you know that accept-
ing it will ease your mind, calm your spirit,
and even whet your appetite for growth.

Are you ready? I know you can handle
it, though not everyone can. Here goes:
You are not always right.

I saw you smile, because you
know I'm right – well, about this,
anyway.

Trying to be right about everything
is a load you cannot carry, and the cost is far
more than you can afford. The next time you
look in the mirror, you may want to remind
yourself of this secret.

And I'll tell you another secret – admitting
that you're not always right makes you even
more lovable than you already are – if that's
possible.

If kids never see their parents mess up—if parents never fail—how will children learn to deal with failure in their own lives? And how could anyone ever live without messing up?

—Ron Rose

Gertrude

My son Lincoln and I had been to the town of Frankenmuth, Michigan, to fish. He was about eleven at the time. The town is only about fifty miles from Flint, where we lived, and is nearly world famous for its breweries and for Zenders – a national monument to fried chicken and sauerbraten. It is much less well known for salmon fishing, but that's why we went there. The Clinton River is dammed there, and the Lake Huron salmon collect below the dam.

We drove over right after school, hoping to fish a couple of hours before dark. It was late fall. When we headed home, after a very successful trip, it was cold and dark. We were speeding along a narrow, twisting

Learning Humility

country road, when suddenly, my headlights revealed a white piscovey duck in the middle of the road. I can't imagine what it was doing in the road at that time of night. I thought ducks were like chickens and went to sleep as soon as it got dark – and this one should have. I was going much too fast to swerve, and there was no time to stop. I heard the sickening *whack* and *crunch* of the duck hitting the underside of the car repeatedly.

★

I thought ducks were like chickens and went to sleep as soon as it got dark – and this one should have.

It isn't easy to explain my next action – in fact, it's a little embarrassing – but I have to try, or I can't tell the rest of the story. You need to know me personally, and you need to understand the way I was brought up. In my family –

nothing was ever wasted –
it was a sin to waste.

Gertrude

I turned around and went back to pick up the duck so we could take it home and eat it. It was lying in a heap, sprawled out in obvious death in the middle of ten thousand feathers. I pulled up alongside, reached out my door, picked up the duck, laid it on the floor behind my seat, and headed home once again. I was driving a compact car. It was an Opel with bucket seats.

Lincoln was very quiet as we drove, but completely alert. Normally, he would have been sound asleep after such a day, but the incident with the duck had totally captured his imagination. I noticed that he kept looking behind my seat. A few minutes later, he said,

"Dad, do ducks have souls?"

"No, Son, ducks don't have souls."

★

He thought for a few minutes and then he said, "Dad, is it okay to pray for a duck?"

"What happens to a duck when it dies?"

"We eat it."

Learning Humility

"I mean, where does it go?"

"It doesn't go anywhere. It just *isn't* anymore."

"Oh." He thought for a few minutes and then he said, "Dad, is it okay to pray for a duck?"

"I guess so, but why would you want to?"

"I feel sorry for it."

He lapsed into a thoughtful silence, and I assumed that he was praying. He kept his eyes on the duck, and a few minutes later he spoke again.

"Dad?"

"What, Son?"

"God just answered my prayer; that duck's alive."

"God doesn't do things like that anymore. The duck is dead."

A few minutes passed.

"Dad? Why doesn't God do things like that anymore?"

"Because the age of miracles ceased when the apostle John died."

"Dad, are you sure of that? The duck is alive. I just saw it move."

"No, Son, the duck may have moved from the motion of the car, but that duck is not alive. I know you feel sorry for the duck, and I do, too, and I know you prayed for the duck; but we have to learn to accept bad things in life. *The duck is dead.* You heard it hit the car, didn't you?"

"Yes, but, Dad, the duck just moved again, and it's not the motion of the car. *It's looking right at me.*"

★

"Trust me. I'm your father, and when I tell you that the duck is dead, you can believe me."

"Son, this has gone far enough. You mustn't allow your imagination to run away with you. I've told you that the duck is dead. *It is dead!* No amount of wishful thinking can bring it back. Trust me. I'm your father, and when *I* tell you that the duck is *dead,* you can believe me.

The – duck – is – dead!
Now, I don't want to hear any more
about that duck;
do you understand?"

Learning Humility

"Yes, Sir."

"Quack."

"What was that noise?"

"I think it was the dead duck, Dad."

I turned around, and sure enough, there was the duck, standing up and looking rather puzzled by its new surroundings.

"Son," I said, "the age of miracles just started again, because that duck was dead!"

★

"Quack."

"What was that noise?"

"I think it was the dead duck, Dad."

We took it home, fed it, found a marvelous place for it to stay – in our swimming pool, which was closed for the winter anyway – and we named her (I guess it was a her) Gertrude. About a month later we went back to Frankenmuth. We took Gertrude and released her as near to the spot where we had found her as possible and went on our way.

Gertrude

I learned a lesson from Gertrude the duck that day. I learned that I'm not always right. I learned that older isn't always wiser; I learned that sometimes we allow our presuppositions to override obvious facts; and I learned that if I insist on being right and won't even listen to another point of view, I might be forced to acknowledge my fallibility by a loud "Quack" of reality.

★

Learn the grace of laughing at yourself.

The next time you feel compelled to stand your ground, no matter the facts, just remember Gertrude the duck and relax a little. Learn the grace of laughing at yourself. It really isn't so bad to admit that you're wrong —

once in a while.

reflections . . .

_____

_____

_____

_____

_____

_____

_____

_____

_____

_____

_____